You Know You're

Getting Old

When...

Ben Fraser

Illustrations by Roger Penwill

summersdale

YOU KNOW YOU'RE GETTING OLD WHEN…

First published in 2003

Summersdale Publishers Ltd
46 West Street
Chichester
West Sussex
PO19 1RP
UK

www.summersdale.com

Printed and bound in China

ISBN: 978-1-78685-028-7

Substantial discounts on bulk quantities of Summersdale books are available to corporations, professional associations and other organisations. For details contact general enquiries: telephone: +44 (0) 1243 771107, fax: +44 (0) 1243 786300 or email: enquiries@summersdale.com.

To..

From..

You know there was something you
wanted to complain about,

you just can't remember what it was.

Your birthday party gets a little wild and you apologise to the neighbours, only to find out *they hadn't even noticed*.

Life without sex would be tolerable, but life without glasses impossible.

You doze off on the bus, and people think you've *passed away*.

Most of your body hurts.
If any bits don't hurt
it's because they've
stopped working.

You know how to read a map, and
insist on memorising a route before
setting off, despite your children
telling you your phone makes
a perfectly good satnav.

You know everything worth knowing. If only someone would *actually ask you about it*.

'Getting some action'
mainly involves buying
a pack of laxatives.

You find a song that shook the world in the wild days of your youth – in the Easy Listening section of the shop.

There is more hair up your nose
than on your head.

You want people to remember
your birthday but to forget how
many of them you've had.

You used to go to bed
at dawn; now that's
when you get up.

You have to choose between tearing off all your clothes and making passionate love – you haven't the energy for both.

You expect to watch your favourite programme at a certain time, once a week. What's all this about *binge-watching*?

Getting up from the armchair
generally requires more
than *two attempts*.

People start telling you
that you look young...
for your age.

You can keep house plants alive for *more than a month* – in fact, you have house plants that are applying for their pension.

You lose track of your last stubborn dark hair – it's gone over to *the grey side*.

By the time you've had a bit of a rest, you've *forgotten* what it was that tired you out in the first place.

Middle-aged people give up their seats for you on the bus.

Those toys you had as a child
that you buried in the garden
are now *worth a fortune*.

You hear yourself passing
on advice to your children
that your parents gave you.

You actually think about
the cost of going out
for a few drinks and decide
to stay in and watch TV instead.

You can be trusted with a secret because you won't remember it anyway.

You stop looking for products
with a lifetime guarantee
and settle instead for a
five-year guarantee.

You feel a *sense of triumph* when you remember what you went upstairs for.

Your life insurance
premium is higher than your
mortgage payments.

You can remember having
a daily paper delivered.

You get pulled aside at airports due to the amount of metal in your *replacement joints*.

You wish you'd given into temptation a bit more while you had the chance.

Helping little old ladies across the street is no longer a good deed, but what happens whenever you *go out with friends*.

You find yourself repeating
things *over and over*.

You find yourself
repeat... oh, hang on.

You get stopped by
the police for driving too
slow instead of *too fast*.

You've discovered the secrets
of the universe – but you
can't remember them.

You and your friends understand the comparative benefits of various pension schemes – in fact, that's your *favourite topic of conversation*.

It can take you days to
remember where you left the car –
or what it looks like.

Your friends make the papers every week – in the obituaries column.

You feel comfortable telling
everyone you meet exactly
what you think of them.

You wear your hair in
a tight bun – to keep
your face in place.

You may not have many short skirts
or figure-hugging outfits in your
wardrobe these days, but your
Tupperware collection is
second to none.

When the phone rings you've been known to answer the remote control… or any *other nearby object*.

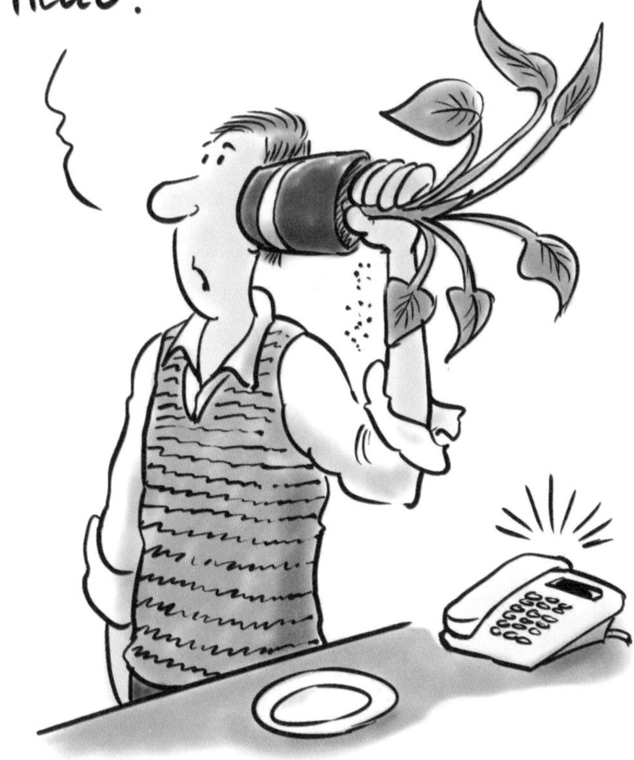
HELLO?
HELLO?

You enjoy hearing about your friends' operations.

Your childhood decades go
from being classified as 'retro'
to *ancient history*.

You use a *mail-order dentist*
– you send them your teeth and
they come back as good as new…

You accept or reject social invitations based on whether they finish '*at a sensible time*'.

You consider 8 a.m.
a good lie in.

You need a hurricane to blow out all the candles on your *birthday cake*.

The car you have now
cost you as much as
your first house did.

You could legally marry
someone half your age.
And they could legally marry
someone *half their age*.

You need a *cine-film projector*
to watch your home movies.

Not wearing a bra causes chafing on your knees.

You start every sentence with,

'This was all fields *when*
I was a child...'

It is no longer possible to get that replacement part for your *gramophone*.

You feel the need to iron
your handkerchiefs.

You dread surprise parties.
Your heart just *can't take it*.

Your family ask casually what kind
of *funeral music* you like.

You no longer see the need for shoes. You have slippers.

Most of your clothes are hand-made – you've *knitted them yourself*.

You find a new passion in your life: the game of bowls.

Your family apologise for *keeping you up* if they phone after dinner.

You find everything on the TV rude, crude or lewd – including the *kids' programmes*.

You sometimes have to think about the answer when someone asks your age.

You get the urge to tell youngsters how much damage they're doing to their feet in *those stilettos*.

You have a selection of
walking stick designs
to match your outfits.

You genuinely think you've
lost your glasses, but they're
on *top of your head*.

You feel no shame in
talking about your bowels
at great length.

You come across a speed hump
while driving and have to reverse
and *take a run-up*.

You have acquired a new language of mutters and tuts, and grunt when you sit down.

The gap between your
belt and your armpits is
considerably smaller
than it used to be.

You spend five hours doing
your weekly food shopping
– plus a good half hour
chatting to the cashier.

Your idea of a wild night
in with your partner is
listening to classical music
with a nice cup of tea.

If you're interested in finding out more about our books, find us on Facebook at **Summersdale Publishers** and follow us on Twitter at **@Summersdale**.

www.summersdale.com